BLACK NAT...

RESURGENCE OF AFRICAN CONSCIOUSNESS

(POCKET EDITION)

Although the author has made every effort to ensure that the information in this book was correct at press time, the author does not assume and hereby disclaim any liability to any party for any loss, damage, or disruption caused by errors or omissions, whether such errors or omissions result from negligence, accident, or any other cause.

BLACK NATIONHOOD

---◊---

ABOUT THE BOOK

HOTEP BELOVED! Caution, this Book "BLACK NATIONHOOD" perhaps, contains information that may stimulate independent thinking.

We must endeavor to embark upon this life-altering voyage of The Resurgence of African Awareness and African Consciousness and culture. Some of you are many moons on this journey.

But, for some, this journey will be challenging, as taking a final exam, while standing on one leg and a barking dog in the background. For others, it will be like trying to walk on a broken leg without the assistance of a pair of crutches.

In any event, successful completion is the only option. For those who are ready, willing to grow, heal, change, and build perhaps this Book will challenge your minds to research and learn about yourselves and the resurgence of African Awareness and Culture.

Black Culture has become this degenerative society where love, peace, joy & the pursuit of happiness is foreign and looks more like the dysfunction of a low-life animalistic society with horrible behaviors.

Many of us weren't taught in School about real African history or culture. It would have enhanced your self-awareness, personal and spiritual growth. Learning who you are and where you originated is imperative for clarity, vitality, and freedom.

This book will challenge you to transform your mind, in efforts to eliminate, upside down, inside out, and backward thinking, of an enslaved mind. It is time to be Free. I challenge you to take this Journey. Much Love to all of you!

BLACK NATIONHOOD

AUTHOR L.P. BALKCOM

Contents

ABOUT THE BOOK 2

BLACK NATIONHOOD 8

IDENTITY 14

RELIGION 22

BLACK ECONOMIC 39

SOCIOLOGY 55

COLOR OF JUSTICE 61

SOLUTION 69

OUT OF DARKNESS LIFE WAS FORMED 85

FINAL THOUGHT 89

ABOUT THE AUTHOR 92

DEDICATION 100

MORE BOOKS 101

BY THIS AUTHOR: 101

BLACK NATIONHOOD

"The Elders of the Village are the boundaries"

~ Ghanaian Proverb

BLACK NATIONHOOD

BLACK NATIONHOOD

What is Consciousness?

Consciousness is the state of being awake and aware of one's surroundings or, the fact of awareness by the Mind of itself and the World.

Consciousness emerges from the operations of the Brain.

What is African Consciousness?

African Consciousness is never denying who you are, first and foremost.

It is knowledge of self and African History. It is when your consciousness is based upon what is right for your race and what you can do to help your race.

Although you have people, who deny being of the African race and want nothing to do with Africans, this can be viewed as committing mental suicide.

The fact of the matter is we are the original Man and the original Woman.

Unfortunately, there were and still are many who do not want you to know this information.

Because, apparently plainly, it is not written in your History book at school.

As Dr. Henrik Clarke stated, "You left your mind in Africa."

Nevertheless, we must find a way to use our minds, to use our African consciousness, culture, and personality as an instrument of power. Although many "Blacks" and or African Americans struggle with feelings of powerlessness, this is indeed an area we must fight to overcome.

Power is necessary for dealing with the World. It is time to reassess and reorganize ourselves, even our personalities, native spirituality, and culture. Believe in the possibilities of mental freedom.

We must believe that we can transform our lives and our situations.

Our African consciousness is not abstract, meaning only existing in thought or an idea but, not having a physical or concrete existence.

Overstand that there are Artifacts around the world that tell a tumultuous story about the deity of our Ancestors. African consciousness is too attainable.

The ideas of Ma'at are always an excellent concrete concept to measure behaviors and test our reality.

BLACK NATIONHOOD

"One foot isn't enough to walk with"

~ Egyptian Proverb

BLACK NATIONHOOD

IDENTITY

What is Identity?

Identity: the fact of being who or what a person or thing is. Or, a close similarity or affinity.

If you are of African descent, you are a Goddess or a God. Overstand that you were stripped of your identity, and spirituality when the Europeans enslaved you. The rotten roots of the corruption of Slavery that shrouded the minds of Africans are still enslaving the minds of African Americans today.

"If you can control a man's thinking you do not have to worry about his action.

When you determine what a man shall think you do not have to concern yourself about what he will do.

If you make a man feel that he is inferior, you do not have to compel him to accept an inferior status, for he will seek it himself.

If you make a man think that he is justly an outcast, you do not have to order him to the back door. He will go without being told; and if there is no back door, his very nature will demand one."

The Miseducation of the Negro by, Carter G. Woodson,

There was an adverse and lasting effect in the minds of many African who have enslaved that bore and raised children. These effects caused by Slavery has trickled down through the generations to you.

The psychological effects subjectively, of refugee survivors.

The trauma endured behind the mass violation of human rights by way of severe torture, displacement, and losses. It left many with challenges with adapting in life with identity issues, attachment, poor nutrition, poor education, safety, and justice. Many of these issues were passed down through generation, to you.

The impact of Slavery stripped us from our native land and gave a piece of paper called a birth certificate, stripped us of our language and our native Spirituality, and gave us English and Christianity. The diaspora of the transatlantic slave trade removed you from your roots thus causing an identity crisis purposefully.

Many had no belongings or heirlooms from their previous lives. If it were not for memories of their heritage, they would not have any connections to their roots, customs, or beliefs.

One could only imagine how the words to old songs sung in their villages and stories told by the elders would escape their memory through all the tortures many had to endure.

Imagine the agony of being packed on ships much like a can of sardines without any clothes covering their body. Some may be their first ride on such a huge vessel while others, being mixed in with different tribes who spoke different languages.

How could one identify with another who spoke an entirely different language?

Of course, this plan was devised by the plantation owners to keep slaves from uniting and plotting against their owners. Slaves were also given European names like Tom and Jerry.

Many old customs like the playing of the drums were banned. They were given "Christianity" as a way of keeping slaves obedient, in order and under control.

There was a Baptist lay preacher by the name of Sam Sharpe who in eighteen thirty-one stirred up a rebellious "Baptist War" in Jamaica.

The Europeans took slaves from Africa to America with no hopes of them ever returning home.

Men, women, and children were expected to work for the rest of their lives under deceptive regimens.

No freedoms or rights would be the fate of many. Slave owners did everything within their sick demented minds to make sure that every slave had no recollection of their language, religion, culture, beliefs, or history.

Who are you?

BLACK NATIONHOOD

"If a stranger comes to stay with you, don't forget when you lay aside his weapons that he is hungry" ~ Maasai Proverb

BLACK NATIONHOOD

―――――― ◈ ――――――

RELIGION

What is Religion?

Religion is the belief in and worship of superhuman controlling power, especially a personal God or gods, a particular system of faith and devotion or, a pursuit or interest to which someone ascribes supreme importance."

Many are not even aware that African people were innately spiritual. Many Ancient Africans understood the laws of Ma'at as being the moral and religious instructions that led the pathway to pursue a life of righteousness, truth, harmony, and justice with self and others.

They understood that there is an unbridled lower self within all human beings. The symbol of this lower self was called Set.

His passionate pursuits of recklessness and impulsiveness are the enemy to controlled urges over the mind, body, and spirit was relentless.

Understanding that the desires of the mind are a representation of the lower self that is often luring the soul into varieties of pleasures and pain in the world of existence.

Desires that would manifest in the forms of selfishness, lust, anger, hatred, greed, and other selfish feelings. These thoughts were considered fetters.

As the Bible mentioned and insisted that "Jesus" breaks every fetter?

Fetter is a kind of restraint.

This mental restraint prevents the soul from discovering, truth, justice, order balance, harmony, and love.

Our thoughts, feelings, and actions should line up with the attributes of and the reflections of our higher self-god.

In Ancient Egyptian mythology, the story of Set, set (Cain) kills Ausar (Abel) out of greed and jealousy. Yes, many stories in the Bible are stories stolen from Ancient Kemet.

He represents the Ego-consciousness within a human that kills the higher self-expression of the Soul.

Basically, African people are born with a moral barometer or compass if I may, that senses right from wrong. Good from the bad.

Once one master the ego it can be a servant to the divine self-expression.

In fact, probably at least eight of the Ten Commandments were stolen from the Ancient Egyptian Principles of Ma'at written at least two thousand years prior.

Do you know who told you that Christianity was the original faith and religion of our ancestors?

Well, they lied to you.

Did you know that in the year 325 A.D, the Roman Emperor Caesar Flavius Constantine called a meeting of bishops and leaders to take place in Nicaea which was an ancient city in Asia Minor?

Constantine called the meeting the Council of Nicaea.

This meeting is where the Roman Empire Declared Christianity, and the Egyptian Mystery Schools closed.

The Council of Nicaea created Christianity and replaced the original African Trinity of Ausar, Auset, and Heru that existed for over four thousand years, with a new trinity of Father, Son, and the Holy Ghost.

It changed world history forever.

Constantine made orders to burn all the original Egyptian mystery books of spirituality. Constantine ordered the closing of all Egyptian temples and mystery schools.

He was the world's very first Christian Emperor.

Egypt was still independent until the coming of Christianity and the start of the Roman Empire.

Know that history has never been the same since the height of the Roman Empire and its declaration of Christianity.

Romans burned down most if not all the books that had ancient teachings and practices for African people.

The Egyptian temples were not just temples of worship for Gods and

Goddesses, but they were also universities of higher learning and enlightenment.

It is also referred to as, mystery schools.

These mystery schools provided extreme enlightenment for Africans and the Mediterranean world. Without them, people were kept in the dark which is what Constantine wanted.

Enlightenment then turned into education, but what is education without enlightenment other than controlled thinking.

Did you know that the original Catholics and Christians were not even allowed to read the Bible or that it was not written in the common language of the people?

Did you know that the mystery schools taught African philosophy, science, and math but, without these basic skills, the average person would be dependent upon the Government?

Clearly, Constantine was a vindictive and hateful person, closing all Egyptian temples and burning down ancient books of teachings.

He was hell-bent on his mission which was to rein his empire with a religion that was designed to fabricate original African spirituality.

It is best never to forgive Constantine for what he did in history, but he must also never be forgotten. He is the sole reason that Africans were written out of religious history as well as world history.

People of African descent are still being controlled daily by the Government and this religion "Christianity."

The Bible continues to keep masses in the dark and away from the light and truth.

Constantine made sure that many religious people would believe that the ancient Egyptian teachings and spirituality are both demonic and evil.

Due to the age of consciousness, a considerable number of people waking up. We must continue to study the original teachings of our ancestors.

Overstanding that enlightenment is far more important than education.

During the transatlantic slave trade, slaves knew their native religion, one thing for sure; slaves did not go without a fight. They rebelled left and right from the moment they were captured all the way across the Atlantic Ocean.

They would damage machinery, or just work extremely slow.

The African slaves on Haiti plantations would pretend to be practicing the slave owner's religion while fusing their African religion with their French owner's Catholic religion thus creating their own type of Christianity called "Vodou."

Many viewed "Vodou" as being this dark religion. In fact, Black people have been programmed to hate anything dark and related to Africa.

Vodou is a creolized religion forged by descendants of Dahomean, Kongo, Yoruba and other African ethnic groups who had been enslaved and brought to colonial Saint-Dominque, which is also known as Haiti where they were "Christianized by Roman Catholic missionaries in the 16th and 17th Dynasty or centuries.

Religion "Christianity" is the leading mind-controlling mechanism ever invented.

In the dictionary when looking up the word "Christianity," there may be many definitions with the words "rumor has it" which is questionable.

Christianity may be defined according to an extraordinary scholar Dr. Ray Hagins as a Euro-gentile psycho-philosophical vehicle of spiritual and intellectual enslavement which has as its end of three things:

The first goal is the cultural and racial superiority of the people who created it. The second thing is the paralysis of analysis by Christianity.

It means you just do not think nor exercise your critical thinking faculties when it comes to Religion.

People say things that do not get questioned or challenged.

The third goal is the perpetual empowerment of the agenda intended by "Christianity."

It is crucial for those who have been misled to see things correctly. One must have a clear analytical understanding of the origin, strategies, and mechanic of the purpose and methods of the device of Christianity that has blinded you in the first place.

Freedom comes when understanding who you are, and we must learn to exercise our intellectual vigilance if we want mental freedom.

Nicaea 325 A.D. is where "Jesus" was created. (The Roman Catholic Ecumenical Council that created Jesus) A. D. stands for Anno Domini which is Latin, and it means (In the year of our Lord).

It doesn't stand for "After the death of.

The Gregorian calendar has been completely adjusted around the existence of this made-up "Jesus." Surely, we have been in existence for more than 2015 years. In fact, according to the Ancient Africa Calendar, after the founding of Kemet AFK, we should be in the year of 6755."

What do you believe?

BLACK NATIONHOOD

"A King's child is a Slave elsewhere."

~ Zimbabwean Proverb

BLACK NATIONHOOD

BLACK ECONOMIC

What is Black Economics?

It is a means that seeks to ensure broader and meaningful participation in the economy by black people to achieve sustainable development and prosperity and to put an end to financial inequality between blacks and whites.

Perhaps, doing some research would give you a better understanding of the economics of this country. The local county state-federal system of law, social justice, education, and health perhaps will not get better for anyone regardless of money and or financial status and education including levels of consciousness.

The underlying motive of the enslavement of Africans was to divide and conquer through the bureaucracy of separatism and colonialism.

As the old saying goes, "United we stand, divided we fall.

If an economic system is not using anything related to increasing self-sufficiency and community restructuring or helping the less fortunate with means to create their own shelter, food, energy, to maintain or gain education and good health. Then, that may be viewed as imploding the system before it is annihilated.

Black Economics is extremely important for survival.

Although Blacks were never taught after slavery the importance and the enlightenment of seeking knowledge, understand, and wisdom regarding spiritual, mental, and economic conditioning the black race.

Many have grown up in the codependency of slavery.

Accepting jobs, food, clothing, and shelter from the slave master was how their minds were trained.

Oftentimes, seeking loans from a capitalist system was the norm and basically still is today. Paying interest on every dollar borrowed. Even though, this nation was built on the backs and sweat of African slaves.

That square piece of paper…Your birth certificates are viewed as some quid pro quo.

Being owned by the Federal Reserve alone has a significant impact on one's psyche. Kind of leaves you feel like you are a part of some Matrix when you find out that no one's birth certificate is an original.

The truth is stranger than fiction.

Serial numbers printed on special Bank Bond Paper and authorized by the American Bank Note Company???

So, let us understand what happen... Back in 1913, the U.S. was short of cash. With war cost by the end of W.W.I, the treasury was depleted, and financial panic occurred.

Money needed to be printed to restore confidence but, they did not have enough equity the economy needed to get back on its feet.

In order to borrow money that one needs... they need collateral.

In 1913 there was nowhere for the United States to go so, they created the Federal Reserve Act.

The FRB regulated how much the U.S. could borrow and put back in circulation with expectations of being repaid like any loan.

After twenty years things got worse and during Franklin D. Roosevelt, 1933 the U.S. was unable to pay when the banks demanded their money.

Thus, He decided to use the people of the U.S. It is too much to go into but, bottom-line...

your original naturalization record is on file in Washington D.C., and you got a copy, and your assets and property are pledged as collateral for National Debt.

That is enough to make you pop a Xanax.

So, to summarize, basically, your identity was kidnapped and move unlawfully to federal territories and therefore enslaved you to a franchise contract for life.

How does this affect your life today?

It is the job of the Elite in White America to keep our people like cattle pawns, controlled under the Banner of Christianity.

Even your "Bibles" say:

Ephesian 6:5 - Slaves obey your earthly masters with fear and trembling, with a sincere heart, as you would Christ.

Colossians 3:22 - Slaves, obey your earthly masters in everything; and do it, not only when their eye is on you and to curry their favor, but with sincerity of heart and reverence for the Lord.

1 Peter 2:18 Slaves, in reverent fear of God, submit yourselves to your masters, not only to those who are

good and considerate but also to those who are harsh.

Matthew 5:38-40 You have heard that it was said, 'An eye for an eye, and a tooth for a tooth (39) But I tell you, do not resist an evil person; but whoever slaps you on your right cheek, turn the other to him also. (40) If anyone wants to sue you and take your shirt, let him have your coat also.

Control a man's thinking you do not have to worry about his action.

The deception is so deep until many are dumb to the fact that the very first Slave Ship was known as:

"The Good Ship Jesus"

Did you know that in two-thousand and three, a government official had a lot to say primarily about the Federal Reserve and still in two-thousand and fifteen not much has changed within the economy perhaps because another government official was being vague and hard of hearing?

The concerns were that the wealthy are out of touch with the needs of the "middle class" which really does not exist and the working-class families

and citizens of the United States of America were the topic in that meeting. He expounded on the fact that the wealthy and the elite only see their primary function and or

BLACK NATIONHOOD

responsibility as the need to represent large, wealthy corporations.

It was clear that this government official and all of his cohorts just did not understand what was going on in the real world with real people.

He even suggested that he come and visit the ordinary people of a particular region to regain his

the perspective of how working-class citizens actually live.

The elite are obviously only interesting in the country clubs and cocktail parties which really are not really America.

Millionaires and billionaires are an exception to the rule.

With the vast amount of jobs lost in the private sector, this is not improving the economy. Unemployment had tripled and is growing higher.

There are trillions of dollars in national debt. Millions had lost their health insurance while billions of geriatrics cannot afford their prescription medication.

Middle-class families were then and pretty much still are in dire straits and cannot send their kids to college.

People are filing bankruptcy at alarming rates.

Business investments are a thing of the past. CEO of Company's makeover five hundred times more than their employees.

There is really no more middle class.

There is a massive gap between the rich and the poor within an economy that supposedly is improving.

What would these stats be if the economy were sinking?

It is a direct insult to tens of millions of American workers who are continually seeking higher wages.

The government continues defending the minimum wage while the elite gets raises and tax breaks. Every year these so-called Elite reach a new low.

They are not really interested in manufacturing in America. Many manufacturing jobs were lost.

This country is upside down, inside out and backward when Walmart has replaced one of the largest Car manufactures GM. This country is paying people starvation wages rather than living wages, and it really does not matter to the Elite.

Thirty cents an hour in another country in appose to thirty bucks an hour in one of the United States to manufacture merchandise.

Unfortunately, other countries have a much high standard of living than the United States. Regarding decent-paying jobs, health care, and education.

Advanced technology does not make much of a difference when people cannot feed their families.

The epiphany is that this government ideology is flawed of how the real world works.

BLACK NATIONHOOD

"The Bee is the doctor of the flowers."

~ Congolese Proverb

BLACK NATIONHOOD

---◇---

SOCIOLOGY

What is Sociology?

Sociology is the study of the development, structure, and functioning of human society and the research of social problems.

Well, let us go back for starters perhaps those whom black people thought was their leaders end up being three defenders of the same faith that European Powers chose to

personally keep our people's minds enslaved.

Dr. King Jr. whose real name was "Michael" and not "Martin Luther."

Henceforth, "King Martin Luther" is the Caucasian founder of Protestantism.

Halie Selassie & Nelson Mandela are also an intricate part of the few that were chosen.

But, ask yourself of what "faith" were they to defend? Was its Christianity?

The "Organization of African Unity" (OAU) was established by Haile Selassie and Kwame Nkrumah in May 1963 in Addis Ababa, Ethiopia, and was dubbed a "Dictatorship" because it failed to protect the rights and liberations of the African People.

In July 2002, it was replaced by the (AU) African Union, in the 1990s under the leadership of Libyan head of state Muammar al-Gaddafi although he was never recognized for his vision and endeavors put into the AU.

Many leaders were thought to be put in place to protect the rights and liberations of African people perhaps.

Let us just say that, the Civil rights era was not for all black.

"Some Africans American believes they could establish a separate, peaceful space within European dominated territory. They were misled to believe a deed, and timely mortgage payments and tax payments will ensure that Europeans will allow them to exist in peace.

They were deceived to expect that Europeans will respect their earnest efforts as good, law-abiding citizens to purchase land so that they can grow their own crops, develop their resources for themselves and become more spiritually connected in peace with no possible threat of invasion.

For some strange reason, they believe that the Europeans had changed.

African American people, racism is very much alive.

African Americans must stop blindly holding on to hope in a world of nonexistent morality.

Never forget these Europeans have done everything they could to conquer power and historical things that did not belong to them. Understand that people unable to defend themselves to keep their power, and land, are still powerless people which could potentially make angry people.

BLACK NATIONHOOD

"More precious than our children, are the children of our children"

~ Egyptian Proverb

BLACK NATIONHOOD

COLOR OF JUSTICE

What is Justice in an injustice society?

Well, it is described as "just" behavior or treatment.

How can there be "Justice" when there is so much injustice in the world hidden in all shapes, forms, and sizes?

This system is and has been ever since the Europeans took over, upside down, inside out and backward.

The deceptive injustice is real.

Just how deep does the rabbit hole go.

Leonard Noisette quoted in Reducing Racial Disparities in the Criminal Justice System (2000) "A justice system which tolerates injustice is doomed to collapse."

At long last, they have bodycams and videotape to prove the injustice of police officers senselessly killing Black men, women, and children on the city streets and or in a local jail.

But, in an unjust society, many of the officers are acquitted of the offense.

Maybe one or two are convicted via the federal court system.

When racial discrimination permeates the judicial system, it is super awkward for people of color to get justice.

It is apparent that the legal system was invented by white men to protect the white interest and to keep the blacks down.

The system is perhaps, characterized by second-rate legal help for black defendants, biased jurors, and judges who discriminate in sentencing.

Studies show statistical inequalities between whites and blacks in arrest rates, imprisonment, and other areas of criminal justice.

Sociologists, too, have suggested that the apparent inequalities have more to do with poverty than race. Street crimes such as robbery and assault, prominent in the statistics, are usually committed by people from poor backgrounds.

The connection between poverty and crime has long been noted. During the nineteen-thirties, a much larger part of the white population was poor, and whites committed a higher percentage of street crime.

The question of poverty alone may well account for many of the apparent inequalities in the system.

Just to give a brief synopsis of the alarming statistics:

The researchers at "RAND" found that black defendants seemed to be treated more harshly at critical points such as sentencing.

But the researchers did not identify a cause for these inequalities. As of 2014, by age 18, 30 percent of black males, 26 percent of Hispanic men and 22 percent of white men have been arrested.

By age 23, 49 percent of black males, 44 percent of Hispanic males and 38 percent of white males have been arrested.

Today, according to NAACP, African Americans now constitute nearly one million of the total 2.3 million incarcerated population African Americans are incarcerated at nearly six times the rate of whites.

About 14 million Whites and 2.6 million African Americans report using an illicit drug.

Five times as many Whites are using drugs as African Americans.

Yet, African Americans are sent to prison for drug offenses at ten times the rate of Whites

Nationwide, African Americans represent 26% of juvenile arrests, 44% of youth who are detained, 46% of the youth who are judicially waived to criminal court, and 58% of the youth admitted to state prisons (Center on Juvenile and Criminal Justice).

These numbers may be approximate but, nevertheless… Something has to change.

BLACK NATIONHOOD

"A Bird that allows itself to be caught will find a way of escaping."

~ Cameroonian Proverb

BLACK NATIONHOOD

SOLUTION

From both sides, the violence, hate, fears, and jealousy all stem from the residual effects of slavery that has been passed down through each generation to you, on both sides.

They are careful, not to sound insensitive about all the innocent deaths, etc. Perhaps the root cause of violence in the Black communities has been the efforts to survive in a system that is upside down, inside out and backward.

Young and old alike are hustling trying to get that illegal money by any means necessary to feed and provide the basic necessities for their families.

First and foremost, one must understand that the positive change in the Black community starts with you.

Speak to your inner self because only you can make the necessary changes that need to happen in your life, family, and community. Do not look for the masses to change first because only you can change yourself. So, contrary to this popular belief of a white system, the inner and the outer you matter.

There appears to be only one solution to freeing we from this system, and that is the restricting of a global economy. We must gradually lessen our participation in this system. The religious systems, jobs, schools, stores, and taxes and come together and build a new existence for us that will ultimately bring the African culture back where we are living once again off the sources of nature.

Another idea has skilled workers in place to update our information system after we have created our own technology.

Also, maintaining domestic and a global economy with our own currency, which is backed by our personal wealth, is also relevant.

The goal is to affect the one point one trillion dollars or more that have not been equally distributed over the last two thousand years. It is time for a change.

African Americans must rid themselves of offices and titles and names. We have too many chiefs and not enough Indians so; there will be any chiefs or Indians. All must unite as one.

Let run some figures.

If 20,000 people give $100 is $2 million. If done monthly by the end of the year you will have $24 million. If done in a three-year plan will have $72 million

Understand that the amount that you pay for a year could perhaps set you up for a lifetime of wealth and happiness.

These funds could go towards a structure that provides African Americans families a lifetime of energy, food, shelter, education, free health, and dental care, etc.

Each building structure will span over no less than 40 acres and will accommodate the 20,000 and their family. It could perhaps be the center of learning and employment of that 20,000.

The plan will then be perpetuated until all African Americans are accommodated.

Do you think this plan is Farfetched, a Pipe dream or Utopia? Well, it is not. This plan is a serious and very well thought out plan by many others before of equality and one of social justice in its purest form.

Since trust is an issue that African Americans must work on eliminating when it comes to business adventures with each other. Then, everyone could receive a full invoice monthly of every dime received and spent.

There will be no waiting games or gimmicks when questions arise. The sole purpose is to erase the worry of living and focus solely on self-community and global economic independence and growth while creating a positive environment.

In this world, African Americans are faced continuously with urban violence and the many faces of poverty.

The majority of minorities deal with structural inequality, institutionalized racism, and police brutality within their communities and cities every day.

Rebuilding African American communities as a unit will hopefully decrease violence, poverty, unemployment, etc., by a considerable percentage.

Every chance one gets it should be to take a more in-depth look into the social, cultural, and political issues which are affecting the African American community and strive to make that change.

Speaking about a group of people, the masses, or race, as though the individual has no importance is all wrong. In any action, it is only the individual that matters. Each one is teaching one.

Any right actions or important decisions, like the search for mental freedoms, the inquiry after truth, can only come from the individual that understands.

If an African American is genuinely an individual of substance, in the sense that he or she is trying to understand the whole process of elevating his or her mind then, he or she will be a creative entity, a free person, unconditioned, capable of pursuing truth for self and not for a result for self but, for everyone involved as a whole.

It is time for African Americans to do for themselves by themselves. Of course, it will be challenging, and more likely than not, Europeans may not like the separatism.

However so, one must be diligent in seeking mental and physical freedom nonviolently in its totality from white supremacy in America.

If mental and physical freedom is not real than perhaps, nothing on earth is real. Maybe even the creator had to use an artificial method rather than original thoughts to create.

Are you the creator?

Then, create your world of freedom.

Perhaps, all things outward of yourself are only a reflection of your own imagining of yourself in your head.

Perhaps everything is but a memory in your life and is flashing nanoseconds before your eyes.

Inner stand you have an intrinsic factor within that helps you to see corruption in a corrupt world. So, trust what you are seeing happening around you on a daily basis, and that is an awakening of a people.

Maybe some were born with this gift of discernment thus seeing becomes easy. Plainly the Ancestors could see clearly.

What did this age-old song really mean?

"Row, row, row your boat, gently down the stream, merrily, merrily, merrily, merrily, or (merely) life is but a dream.

Could this song be merely telling up to your thoughts steadily or gently down the stream of consciousness, simply and happily because, this thing called life or reality is an illusion?

Our ancestors showed us the example of love they gave us every example we needed to know. Those examples we did not see with our eyes, we must gather them from our hearts.

We are Gods.

We are the creator of reflection.

Most people are not ready to accept the responsibility and the liability of stepping up to the challenge. Most will worry about self and family instead of adopting a village state of mind.

One must Inner standing that the whole has success because of the whole works together.

Believing that it is possible to create a structure that will be self-sufficient, that would focus on a global scale economy which means accumulating a potential for substantial wealth for multiple people with plenty of lands large enough for wildlife.

It is time to rid yourselves of the slave master's centuries-old disillusionment that has poisoned ninety-nine percent of your mental. Past steppingstones were non-effective.

Their food and European education have poisoned your minds. Pineal glands are inoperable in this state. It has become illegal not to accept their healthcare. No one without employment has dental care. Yet, they refuse you adequate housing and shelter in their communities.

It is a system where you are trying to get justice from, will never be granted equality because it is perhaps unjust.

It is merely to let it go and come together to build for yourselves by yourselves. Bring your African village culture and spirituality back.

Or, remain under the rule and reign of a myth of white supremacy, European nation, and be destroyed under the control of another.

BLACK NATIONHOOD

"Water that has been begged for does not quench the thirst"

~Soga People of Uganda

BLACK NATIONHOOD

OUT OF DARKNESS LIFE WAS FORMED

"Out of darkness life is formed and brought forth into the light.

One enters into a realm of the unknown but, only for a moment. Soon, life begins to happen all around you.

You begin to see, know, and learn. Enemies start to surround you. Chaos and harsh terrains of emotions overshadow you. Tricks and gimmicks try to overtake you.

Sadness and confusions try to overpower you. But still, you grow.

Through the mental blindness and deafness, you continue to see, hear, and breathe, although sometimes you feel breathless.

But then there is this voice you here coming up from inside you,

telling you not to fear cause, your Ancestors are near.

There this strength rising to the top of your head. Again, this voice you hear telling you to tell the people they are going to win if they build this structure in the shape of a womb "O," from the outside within.

For in this shape they will never again be tossed out, shaken up or broken."

The poem was written by:

Author LaTonya Page-Balkcom

BLACK NATIONHOOD

AUTHOR L.P. BALKCOM

FINAL THOUGHT

Inner stand that the Myth of white supremacy is the nature of the enemy that will perhaps try to enslave your mind and spirit and have you blindly raising your children in a racist system society.

Perhaps try to gain the knowledge to destroy the mental and physical holds of the enemy and embrace the wisdom necessary to re-build your life independent of this system.

Learn and understand how to obtain balance. If you want to survive, you will fight spiritually and mentally for your life and freedom.

Fight for the five primary functions of life, the welfare of your family, your food, energy, education, shelter, health, and dental.

Feed my people, energize them, educate them, shelter them, and provide them with free healthcare and dental care, says the Ancestors.

BLACK NATIONHOOD

"The humble pay for the mistakes of their leaders" ~ Tanzanian Proverb

ABOUT THE AUTHOR

Author L.P. Balkcom is a brilliant Autochthon-American, self-published author based out of Illinois, a loving mother of one, and a grandmother of five loving children.

Author L.P. Balkcom officially began her writing career as a hobby in the late nineties. Her focus was on several genres, but mainly Romance/Drama Novella. Writing in Multi-Genres, allowed her to insert a positive message that would have a positive IMPACT on the readers from different lifestyles and backgrounds, rather than one type.

Author L.P. Balkcom's books offer diverse audience minds to flow

freely, without judgment, while reading stories that are relatable, and easy to make the connection between characters. Perhaps, even learn something new.

Author L.P. Balkcom bestseller "MAÀT 42 PLUS GOD," only reference Ancient Kemetic Spirituality as an alternative to institutional Religions.

MAÀT is not a Religion, but merely a way of Life.

She focused on Ancient Kemetic Spirituality and understanding the 42 Negative Confessions/Concepts/Principles of MAÀT because they existed 2000 years before the Ten Commandments. She shared her findings in a book, hoping to enlighten ALL people, but mainly colonized melanated people. These Concepts were practiced by our Ancient African Ancestors, as Spirituality.

In May of 2015, she self-published "MAÀT 42 Plus God."
"God," meaning "The Totality of Creation Itself."
"Colors of Consciousness," and more books followed.
All Books are now available on her website: WWW.MAAT42PLUSGOD.COM also, Amazon, Kindle, Barnes & Noble, etc., as a Paperback book and eBook.

What inspired Latonya to write her Bestseller, "MAÀT 42 Plus GOD?"

Growing up under the auspices of

Institutional Religion, the constant condemnation, and judgment, life felt inhibiting, stifled, and restrictive. Thus, the search began for a Spirituality less debilitating, and more liberating. She came across the teachings of MAÀT, an Ancient Kemetic Spiritual Concept, that promotes Love, Truth, Justice, Reciprocity, Balance, Order, and harmony.

She began to practice & apply the 42 Principles of MAÀT, and her Spiritual life flourished in many positive ways. It was the reintroduction to MAÀTIAN principles, blossomed from African Spirituality rather than, the falsehoods that misrepresent true Spirituality that gave her a new vision on life.

Author L.P. Balkcom's book "MAÀT 42 Plus GOD," is NOT a Scholarly History Lesson, but rather to be read, viewed, and perhaps, considered, a "Heart Lesson."

African Spirituality DOES NOT condemn others but stresses to maintain the purity of your own heart. Asé

Author L.P. Balkcom is determined to leave her imprint on the Publishing World. She offers a wide range of books for adults, and children, with great topics that encourage self-awareness, self-empowerment, self-expression, self-determination, and African Spirituality.

Books that offer clarity and

perhaps, guidance on how to live a more balanced and prosperous life.

Coming from a life of Pain to Prestige, Author L.P. Balkcom is brilliant, smart, witty, self-taught, well-versed on many topics, and subjects.
Seldom does she operate without a Spirit of Excellence and her discernment, most would say is on point.

Latonya desires to become the next World-Renowned Author for a new generation of readers. Only you can make her dreams a reality.

Thank you for reading my books.

If you would like to purchase books or invite.

Author Latonya Page-Balkcom

to your special event, please call:

702-218-2970

Or visit:

WWW.MAAT42PLUSGOD.COM

Email: maat42plusgod@yahoo.com

BOOK REVIEWS ARE WELCOMED

www.amazon.com/-/e/B00ZPUYXF8

BLACK NATIONHOOD

"Discord between the Powerful is a fortune for the poor" ~ *African Proverb*

DEDICATION

Dedicated to my mom,

Ernestine Jones-Page

who transitioned April 18, 1991, R.I.P.?

Also, to my father, Herman Page Sr.,

for without you, there would be no me

To my daughter Iiesha Ernestine

Thanks for keeping me grounded

Also, to my grandchildren,

Mia Simone, Martin (Marty) William Jr, Ivy J. Latonia, Constance Joy, and Quentin Carter.

Thanks for being the Sunshine in my Life every day.

MORE BOOKS BY THIS AUTHOR:

MA'AT 42 PLUS GOD

AKASHA & YOU

REWIRE THE BLACK MIND TO PROSPER

COLORS OF CONSCIOUSNESS

NO MORE HOOKUPS

WORDS OF A POETIC GODDESS

FICTION/DRAMA/ROMANCE

3 Book Series

SPIRIT OF REJECTION Book 1

SPIRIT OF LESBIANISM Book 2

FROM PAIN TO PRESTIGE Book 3

CHILDRENS BOOK

ANCIENT EGYPTIAN GODS, MYTHS, AND SYMBOLS

SPIRIT LED APPROACH TO PARENTING

MICKEY, MS. PENELOPE & ME

PLEASE RETURN TO AMAZON
BOOK REVIEWS ARE WELCOMED

OR VISIT MY WEBSITE:

WWW.MAAT42PLUSGOD.COM

BLACK NATIONHOOD

THANKS FOR READING!

BOOK REVIEWS ARE WELCOMED

Made in the USA
Las Vegas, NV
23 February 2024